home altars

of mexico

Home Altars of Mexico

Photographs by Dana Salvo

Essays by Ramón Gutiérrez, Salvatore Scalora, William Beezley

Afterword by Amalia Mesa-Bains

Thames and Hudson

First published in Great Britain in 1997
by Thames and Hudson Ltd, London

Copyright © 1997 by Dana Salvo
Essays © by the University of New Mexico Press

British Library Cataloguing-in-Publication Data
A catalogue record for this book is available from the British Library
ISBN 0-500-28019-3

Printed and bound in Hong Kong

Frontispiece: Rosha Lacruz and her two small children
by their modest home altar, Zinacantan, Chiapas.

CONTENTS

Preface: A Family Album *Dana Salvo* 1

ALTARS OF SAN JUAN CHAMULA AND ZINACANTAN, CHIAPAS 7

Introduction *Ramón A. Gutiérrez* 17

EVERYDAY ALTARS 21

Conjuring the Holy: Mexican Domestic Altars *Ramón A. Gutiérrez* 37

MEMORIAL AND DEVOTIONAL ALTARS 49

Flowers and Sugar Skulls for the Spirits of the Dead *Salvatore Scalora* 63

ALTARS FOR DAY OF THE DEAD 81

Home Altars: Private Reflections of Public Life *William H. Beezley* 91

NACIMIENTOS 109

Afterword *Amalia Mesa-Bains* 123

A CURANDERO'S HOME 129

Acknowledgments 136

To Dawn

for being the heart and soul of this work

and to Jahna and Simone

for inspiring friendship and affection

PREFACE

a family album

Dana Salvo

Traveling through small rural hamlets in Mexico the past decade, I have witnessed the traditional lifestyles of its native people. In the midst of meager and humble conditions I have found an oasis of spiritual wealth and visual opulence.

Within the small thatched houses of these Mayan descendants, houses sometimes made only of interwoven sticks covered with mud, I have found walls and entire rooms ritually decorated with makeshift altars honoring both the memory of their ancestors and the birth of Jesus. These altars also chronicle life's ebb and flow of births and deaths, plantings and harvests, and sickness and health.

Animist symbolism, Christian imagery, crucifixes, family mementos, faded photographs, votive candles, blinking lights, balloons, fruits, an occasional TV, dolls, images from popular culture, the flag, and calla lilies are all assembled against peeling backdrops of pastel pinks, blues, and greens. Typically these modest one-room dwellings serve a variety of functions: being both the family bedroom and living area, as well as the kitchen, granary, and closet.

In the highlands of Chiapas, while traveling with my wife, Dawn, and our eight-month-old baby daughter, Jahna, we first caught a glimpse of the dazzling decorations and vernacular iconography that adorned the small domestic spaces inhabited by such large families.

We had arrived in Chiapa de Corzo in mid-December, as each family and member of the town was preparing for the Christmas holidays. The markets were alive with color, filled with little Biblical clay figurines, painted wooden mangers, hand-crafted toys, and a wide array of foods, mostly sweets—candied fruits, colored sugar treats, and nuts. We quickly learned that the candies were particularly significant as piñatas were exploding in numerous households each evening creating a Heaven on Earth for the town's young children.

Beginning on December 16 and continuing each evening until Christmas Eve, groups of children take part in *Las Posadas*. The Posada is a traditional procession of young children reenacting the story of Mary and Joseph seeking shelter at the inn. Scores of children dressed in Biblical costumes, carrying candles and a small platform bearing tiny figures of Mary and Joseph, march from door to door singing songs, begging to be let in. At last, when the door is opened to the weary travelers, a festive party for all begins. The cul-

Top to bottom:
A typical stick and mud house in Yucatán.
Three generations of a Mayan family.
Jahna at eight months old with other Mayan children.

mination occurs when the young children wildly break the piñata with sticks. We were warmly invited to participate in these festive gatherings. The doors to homes were opened wide for us.

The images reproduced on the following pages depict the many remarkable environments, or worlds of wonder, we have since witnessed upon passing the threshold. Each family we encountered had a genuine affection for our daughter Jahna. Only an infant, very fair, with curling blonde hair and an infectious smile, Jahna would be whisked to the center of the home and embraced by all the women. Dawn and I were deeply touched by the warmth and generosity of spirit that was extended to us during those initial days. That spirit has continued to characterize our subsequent visits.

In the years to follow, our family, which has grown to include another daughter, Simone, has made many pilgrimages to Mexico. Simone, with different colored eyes of deep blue and brown, is treated as a small goddess. Jahna, now twelve, has swung her stick alongside dozens of Mexican friends at a wide assortment of piñatas. We have come to realize that nearly every day becomes a holy day in a land which celebrates life.

Top to bottom:
Don Filogonio Perez, with Dawn holding baby Simone, and Jahna.
Baby Simone and Dana Salvo with Octavio, San Juan Chamula, Chiapas.
Jahna with Chamulan children holding baby Simone.

We have visited the shrinking numbers of Purépechan Indians in Michoacán, the Chamulan and Zinacantan communities in Chiapas, the Zapotecs of Oaxaca, the Mayan of Yucatán, and a host of groups scattered along the many miles we have traveled. While the material comforts in evidence may be few, the familial and spiritual existence is rich, by standards other than monetary, comprising a highly complex and sophisticated social and religious system.

My family and I have been quite fortunate in having been allowed the rare privilege to spend time contemplating these personal domestic environments, and later to be allowed to photograph the shrines that occupy a place of prominence within each home. Many cultures do not always warm to the outsider, and often regard photographers as bandits who "steal the soul" as they snap away with a camera.

In mountain villages of Chiapas, such as San Juan Chamula and Zinacantan, warnings strictly prohibiting photography are posted for all to see. Penalties for violating these laws can be stiff and harsh: a confiscated camera, being pelted with stones, fruits, and vegetables, and even landing in jail can be the consequences of such a trespass.

Top to bottom:
Jahna, age five, pulling the slide of a film holder to make an exposure.
Jahna, age eight, in a cemetery, checking an exposure with Polaroid film.
Children looking through the ground glass of a view camera.

As I did not work with cameras hanging from my neck, which I could easily point and shoot, I never experienced hostility or suspicion. Instead, Dawn and I and our children were treated with friendship and compassion and were welcomed into people's homes.

After we came to know one another as families, our new friends would learn we were artists. I would show examples of my work and explain how making a photograph required the better part of half a day. Most were eager to see the production and to have an image created of their home.

Being huddled beneath a black cloth looking through an elegant wooden view camera at a world that is upside down and backward added a special dimension to the picture-making event. Because I used Polaroid professional instant sheet film, I was able to pull an image from the paper within minutes of an exposure, thereby generating an enormous amount of enthusiasm.

It would often be hours before I exposed the final negative. The time involved, along with the closeness of space and the reverential nature of the altars, transformed the photographic process into a collaborative undertaking. During that time we sat by women cooking over open fires, preparing soups and corn tortillas, while hearing family stories, dreams, and folktales. We

Top to bottom:

In the village of Zinacantan, I would initially set up to photograph the people who were curious about our arrival. Later, as more people gathered, I would begin to visit houses.

Delivering prints to a family on a return visit to Chiapas.

Jahna, age twelve, and Simone, age seven.

watched at ceremonies as men drank *posh,* a potent sugarcane liquor, while eating bread and red chili peppers. We learned about the life of corn and saw the parallels between the planting and harvesting cycles of this crop and the family's traditions.

We were able to witness a healing ceremony where a shaman tied back the wings of a chicken and, using the bird as a brush, stroked the body of the inflicted, all the while chanting and singing. We were able to glimpse these small vignettes into another world because as families we had common ground and much to share.

In addition to photographing home interiors, I also made family portraits. The Polaroids, and the enlargements I would bring back on subsequent visits, became treasured objects which would quickly find a place of significance within the house. In offering these photographs as gifts to each family, we were able in some way to return their kind affection. As our visits to San Juan Chamula and Zinacantan formed so much of our impressions of Mexico, so too, then, these pages begin with photographs I was privileged to make in these villages.

altars of san juan chamula
and zinacantan, chiapas

1. Flowering bromeliads, suspended from the rafters, frame and enclose this Chamulan shrine. An air plant, these flowers will last for months. Tamed and manned bull-shaped candle-holders face the saints found behind this unusual partition.

2. Several varieties of corn are suspended from the rafters in this Chamulan home with a house cross in the kitchen.

3. Rosha Gonzalez sitting beside her table altar covered with pine needles, flowers, and saints, Zinacantan.

4. Ceremonial banners hang from the rafters above the Zinacantec family shrine of Yuxep Hernandez. This arch of palm and pine boughs, framing the holy images, is flanked by handcrafted traditional instruments: a two-stringed violin, ritual harp, and guitar. On the floor covered with pine needles are the spotted jaguar candleholders, copal incense burners, and bottle of *posh*, a powerful sugarcane liquor.

5. Four boughs of pine, symbolizing the four corners of the Mayan world, surround the house cross of this Chamulan family. They proudly display the staff, held by the man, indicating their responsibility to the community for organizing an upcoming religious festival.

6. In the sixteenth century, following the Spanish conquest of Mexico, the Catholic clergy ordered the Maya to honor Christ's redemptive cross. Chamulan families traditionally place the house cross on the eastern wall for the rising sun. In this example, the painted red wall, symbolizing the blood of Christ and their ancestors, provides a backdrop to three crosses bound together, in the midst of pine boughs and flowers. The crosses were tied together to strengthen their collective healing power.

7. This Christ figure is dressed in a woven garment for warmth on this Zinacantec house shrine.

The dog busts represent the man's animal double, or spiritual companion, as visioned in dreams.

8. A corner altar with images of saints, including St. Theresa, adorned with a starfish halo, icons, toys, TV, and family snapshots.

INTRODUCTION

Ramón A. Gutiérrez

The photographs of home altars that Dana Salvo has gathered here were taken in the southern Mexican states of Chiapas, Michoacán, Oaxaca, Campeche, Quintana Roo, and Yucatán in the late 1980s. These photographs record the private spaces of family life within the household. In each photograph an altar is the central feature of a room. Mexico's Indian and mestizo peoples, in acts of private devotion, regularly construct home altars to commemorate their relations with their ancestral past and their place within a grander cosmic order. On the simplest of these altars, arranged in a hierarchical fashion, are snapshots and portraits of family members, both living and dead, alongside statues and pictures of the spiritual family in heaven—Christ, the Virgin Mary, and a host of angels and saints. Candles, plastic flowers, and personal mementos adorn these domestic shrines. A diploma here, plastic dolls and figurines there, a pillow with two hand prints that reads "I Love You Mother," and food of various sorts are but some of the many offerings and embellishments on these altars. Each portrait and each adornment on an altar has profound personal and familial meanings. When visitors or residents of the household stand before these altars in simple acts of prayer, reflection, and meditation, they place themselves and their family in that grander cosmic scheme of memory and history. In a very profound sense domestic altars are first and foremost family genealogies. Much as altars and altar screens in churches tell the history of the Catholic Church by gathering images of angels and saints, of martyrs and virgins, so too home altars tell intimate personal histories.

The words and photographs by Dana Salvo and the essays by Salvatore Scalora, William H. Beezley, Amalia Mesa-Bains, and myself offer readers dispersed around the globe a window into the private domestic devotions of Mexico's rural populace. Photographs of home altars document acts of religious piety rarely seen by outsiders. In the text and images gathered here is a visual cornucopia of Mexico's religious present and past.

This volume opens with Dana Salvo's essay, "A Family Album," in which he explains the genealogy of his own interest in photographing sacred domestic shrines, how he and his family were welcomed into the spiritual center of Mexican households, and how he created the dazzling and luminous photographs contained herein. In the essay that follows, "Conjuring the Holy: Mexican Domestic Altars," I provide an extended discussion of how Mexican women and men have conjured the holy, how they have invested space and time with sacred meanings, and how those meanings are embodied in shrines. Here too is a discussion of the suppression, fusion, and transfusion of sacred icons and symbols during war, of how victors impose their domination over vanquished enemies, mocking their deities and their gods, simultaneously superimposing a new pantheon of gods. What one sees in Dana Salvo's photographs of Mexican home altars are the products of a spiritual conquest of Mexico's indigenous peoples begun by Hernán Cortés and his Spanish compatriots in 1519. On these altars one sees hybridity, the blending of cultures, traditions, and beliefs produced when two peoples met in conflict and, in the centuries that followed, accommodated themselves to each other.

Mexican home altars and shrines are continuously constructed year-round. But on special occasions, and especially when Christmas and the Day of the Dead draw near, the pious act of building an altar, carefully gathering its important elements, and lovingly adorning it routinely takes place. In his essay, "Flowers and Sugar Skulls for the Spirits of the Dead," Salvatore Scalora delves into the complex signs and symbols that mark the Mexican Day of the Dead celebrations. Death to the Aztecs was the wellspring of life, he explains. Out of the blending of indigenous and European Catholic ideas about the afterlife emerged the modern celebrations of Day of the Dead. Every element of the home altars that Dana Salvo records in his photographs, Salvatore Scalora tries to explain. What is the significance of the fruit arches that adorn so many altars in this book? They represent the heavens, the sun, the moon, and the stars. Why are marigolds so prominently displayed on these altars? Their fragrance guides the spirits of the dead to their ancestral home. What is the meaning of the copal incense that surrounds the altars? How has the American celebration and commercialization of Halloween affected Mexican Day of the Dead observations? These are but a few of the many questions that Salvatore Scalora poses and answers as he contextualizes Dana Salvo's photographs of those altars constructed in honor of the dead.

William H. Beezley's essay, "Home Altars: Private Reflections of Public Life," chronicles the long history of domestic altars and private oratories in Europe, Africa, and America. Beezley describes how during the sixteenth-century spiritual conquest of Mexico's Indians, the Catholic clergy expanded the religious space occupied by churches, while simultaneously seeking to desecrate and eradicate the sites of Indian worship. By necessity, Indian shrines were driven into secret spaces, deep within the household and clearly out of sight of the Catholic clergy. Ironically, though, with the emergence of Mexico as a secular nation at the end of the eighteenth century, the power of the Catholic Church was curtailed. Along with the rise of secular government in the independent Republic of Mexico came the constriction of religious civil space. Where before the Church could display its icons and statues anywhere it deemed fit, even outside sanctuaries, increasingly representatives of the state relegated such displays to church interiors. Lacking priests to minister to the faithful, barred from popular civic spaces by secular-minded leaders, the Mexican Catholic Church capitulated, accepting the need of their Catholic faithful for daily contact with the holy. This need, Beezley argues, is why home altars became so important in Mexico.

The volume ends with the voice of Amalia Mesa-Bains, a contemporary artist involved with and inspired by the tradition of domestic altars. She views Dana Salvo's photographs of household shrines as an accumulation of personal experiences and memories that become a continuous chronicle of family faith and history.

everyday
altars

9. Nuestra Señora de Guadalupe has been given celestial treatment; elevated on a shelf, she floats among the stars, bathed in the amber light of a yellow bulb—the sun, Quintana Roo.

10. In the fishing village of Campeche, a shrine embedded into the wall is in the shape of a boat.

11. A shelf (nicho) honoring the Santo Niño de Atocha and Nuestra Señora de Guadalupe, along with a treasured diploma and an ancestral portrait. The purple cloth knotted to the cross indicates Lenten season, Campeche.

12. Before this altar decorated with pictures of saints and ancestors, corn and husks are placed as offerings and blessings, Chiapas.

13. In the village of Santa Elena, Yucatán, this table supports a box which houses San Isidro, the local patron saint, alongside a broken crucifix. Melon, corn, and *posh* (firewater) are offerings placed to the side. On the left side is stacked firewood.

14. A Christ figure adorned with a necklace and a Virgin of Guadalupe clock, Yucatán.

15. This altar is a collage of family photos, a black angel, St. Theresa, a black panther, a white horse, dolls, and cords, Quintana Roo.

16. A *nacimiento* for the Christmas holidays, in the home of Paula Sanchez. I have visited Paula regularly over the years. Now in her
eighties, she is an enormously gifted and kind woman, whose house is always changing to reflect the seasons and holidays. Here,
a corner table is covered with representations of the Christ Child surrounded by saints and gods, Quintana Roo.

17. The same corner transformed for the Easter holidays. Fluffy cat wrapping paper was a substitute for the Easter bunny.

18. Browned boughs remain from the Feast of San Sebastian, the patron saint of Chiapas.

19. A large household shrine honoring the Santo Niño de Atocha, shown here holding a basket and a gourd, Quintana Roo.

20. A shelf honoring the Santo Niño de Atocha. The stained wall on the right is the result of water damage that occurred when the roof flew off during a hurricane, Quintana Roo.

21. The same shelf one year later.
The folded sheets are evidence of
the woman's job as a laundress.

22. The corn bin often has a prominent place in the house. As corn is the primary food in their diet, icons serve to protect and bless it, Yucatán.

CONJURING THE HOLY

mexican domestic altars

Ramón A. Gutiérrez

Every culture has a palpable sense of the sacred. The ways in which the power of the sacred operates, the places that it inhabits, the objects that it can animate, the existential states that it can induce, everywhere shapes the ways individuals conceive of themselves within larger systems of meaning. Whether in Mexico or New Mexico, whether in the United States of America or the Confederacy of Freely Allied Socialist States, the holy is conjured through the conjunction of space, objects, and time. On holy ground and in places particularly invested with the sacred, men and women of every faith surround themselves with objects they deem to be particularly potent loci of the holy to periodically ritualize their relationships. Such rituals, be they to tie the living with the dead, to bring order to the cosmos, or to promote blessings, prosperity, and peace, are a fundamental part of the fabric of cultures world-wide.

As moderns living in the industrialized countries of the West our sense of the sacred and its link to our sense of personhood is strongly defined by our belief in the power of medicine and of the biological sciences. Life and death, the enhancement of life, and its termination when pain and suffering make it unbearable and senseless to continue, are decisions for which we rely extensively on physicians. We routinely tell the young and the old in our society to visit the doctor once a year, even if one has seemingly good health. There in the sanitized purity of examining rooms and hospitals, through instruments and scopes that allow doctors to interpret the inner working of our bodies, we actively participate in the medical metaphysics that has such primacy in the industrialized West.

In lesser industrialized countries, in places like Mexico where much of the populace is still tied to an agrarian way of life, religion vies very powerfully with science in explaining the general order of things. Rural Mexican peasants make sense of the mysteries of life and death, and of their place in the community of the living and the communion of the dead, through their religious beliefs. Religion punctuates the days of the week, the seasons of the year, the periods of celebration and of fast, and the moments that must be devoted to commemoration and contemplation. At these moments Mexican women and men congregate in homes, in churches, at grave sites, and at shrines with objects invested with the holy. It is at these moments that they believe that they stand at the intersection of the matrices of the cosmic order.

These sites of cosmic conjunction, these instances of ritual remembrance by which the living are conjoined with the dead, and by which humans renew their historical connections to the past and present, make up the world that Dana Salvo has poignantly photographed and recorded herein. This series of complex portraits documents the religious lives of the rural peasantry of southern Mexico. Dana Salvo takes us into the most intimate of sacred spaces—the household—to behold how the holy is imagined and organized therein. In home altars one sees a sense of the sacred that is juxtaposed to the space and altars contained within Roman Catholic churches. The sacred time that Catholic priests commemorate in church when they transform bread and wine into the body and blood of Jesus Christ, is radically different from the familial time remembered when incense, food offerings, and flowers are set out on home altars for ancestral spirits to feed on. Whereas the objects invested with the sacred in churches are statues and relics that tie one to the communion of saints, to the angels and apostles in heaven, and to the history of a church triumphant, on home altars the photographs, trinkets, and mementos construct family histories that visually record one's relations to a lineage and clan.

Dana Salvo's photographs of Mexican domestic altars record a complex web of meanings. Some of those meanings are to be found in the indigenous religions of Mexico's people; others come from Spain's violent imposition of Roman Catholicism through conquest; and still others come from the secular world of modern commerce and politics. The sedimentary levels of history and experience represented by the particular emplacement of objects that adorn these domestic altars are powerfully emotive. Here objects, space, and time combine to conjure the holy. How that holy is constructed, how the indigenous meanings of the sacred were changed by the Spanish conquest of Mexico's indigenous peoples, how Mexico's native peoples clandestinely resisted the coercive imposition of the religious pantheon of their dominators,

Ramón A. Gutiérrez

are the themes we will explore here as an explication and prelude to Dana Salvo's rich photographic text. Only by digging down through these historic layers of meaning and untangling some of the webs of signification can we fully appreciate and understand the power ascribed to home altars in the daily lives of Mexicans.

Before the sixteenth-century imposition of Christianity on Mexico's Indian peoples, a wide array of religious beliefs and practices existed in Mesoamerica. In the northern regions of present-day Mexico where the nomadic Chichimecas eked out an existence through hunting and gathering, religious life was simple, mirroring the basic seasonal rhythms of nature and the tempo of daily life. Spirits animated every living thing. Winter's ferocity as a season was believed to be a result of the character of its spirit, just as the power and velocity of the wind could be explained by its soul. Humans, plants, animals, natural and supernatural forces each had a unique spirit; spirits that were all intricately linked with humans in ties of reciprocity.

Among the indigenous sedentary horticulturalists of central Mexico, similar souls and spirits were deemed to animate the forces of the universe. What made these spirits different from those nomadic peoples imagined was their location in specific places, reflective of the fact that both the farmers' social well-being and that of their crops was tied to a specific ecology and geography. These farmers had a sense of themselves and of the place they inhabited as the center of the universe. These were centers of cosmologies that extended outward to the four directions of the compass, upward to the heavens, and downward to the underworld. Each of these directions was governed by a dominant color: white for the south, red for the north, green for the west, and yellow for the east. Quite commonly natural features in the topography—hills and mountains, plateaus and canyons, rivers and lakes—delimited the topography that people considered sacred. These physical coordinates of the holy were often marked by altars and shrines. For here were sites where humans could communicate with the spirits that animated the universe, sites where offerings, missives, and gifts could be dispatched to the spirits confident that there would be a prompt receipt and sure reply.

Ramón A. Gutiérrez

Enclosing such spaces, constructing walls and edifices around them, and then establishing a priesthood to propitiate the spirits that resided therein, were historical developments that occurred in various places in Mesoamerica. As lineages and clans expanded into powerful states through warfare and conquest, tribal religious beliefs were elevated to the logic of state. The transformation of the Aztecs from a nomadic band of hunters and gathers who foraged in Mexico's north to one of the most powerful states of the Americas is perhaps the best example of this process. Swooping into the Valley of Mexico as ferocious warriors, the Aztecs quickly conquered the prolific sedentary agriculturalists that resided there and harnessed their rich human and natural resources. From the very moment of triumph, the Aztecs, like so many other indigenous groups in the hemisphere, imposed their pantheon of tribal gods and spirits on the peoples they subjugated. They did this not by eradicating the established sacred topographies of the conquered, but through an additive principle, superimposing a set of tribal or official state beliefs atop those of the locale. Sacralizing space in different ways, investing time with new meanings, and adding new objects that were potently invested with the holy was the daily stuff of Mexico's expansionistic tribal past.

The Spanish conquest of America's richest empire, the Aztec state, began in 1519 when Hernán Cortés, with a band of roughly four hundred men, arrived in the Valley of Mexico. By 1521 the Aztecs had been defeated militarily, and by 1524 the twelve Franciscan friars charged with the spiritual conquest of the Indians had begun their work. Much like the Aztecs who had imposed their tribal gods on the peoples they conquered, so too the Spaniards were intent on Christianizing the Indians by imposing their tribal gods, spirits, and beliefs. But unlike the Aztecs, whose cosmology was usually added to the local pantheon through superimposition, the Spanish friars believed that the native ground first had to purified of its "heathen" and "demonic" past.

Purifying the local terrain of its idolatrous past was the work of iconoclasts. Burning icons that represented the ancestral tribal gods, destroying the sacred shrines that were privileged entrees to the holy, and imprisoning the priest purveyors of the pernicious seeds of idolatry, were the activities that occupied the Catholic Church and its clerics in the war that they waged against Satan. But once that ground was cleansed, once the visible manifestations of the devil had been eradicated, the friars superimposed the Christian cosmology, with its own sacred objects, its own geography, and its own sense of time.

When Christians gathered together to celebrate their relations they did so on ground sanctified by Christ's redemptive cross, in the presence of sacred objects, and at times that commemorated the life of Christ or those of the saints. Since reverential objects were the most potent loci of the holy in Christianity, it was primarily through enclosure, through the construction of a church or an oratory, that space received its power. The emplacement of churches was important only when it served a didactic end—when churches were constructed atop the ruins of a razed temple or the shattered walls of a shrine. The sacred objects of greatest power enclosed within a church were the things of divine worship—the Eucharist, tabernacle, altar stone, and images of Christ, of Mary, his mother, and of the saints. The friars brought these sacred objects to Mexico to serve as the focus for the celebration of community. Their mobile quality allowed them to be moved to and fro, to be paraded solemnly through town and countryside, and to be stolen and profaned.

As we will see shortly, in the historical evolution of Mexican Catholicism still practiced to this day, the meanings of home and of the domestic altars constructed therein gained their significance primarily in juxtaposition, and quite often in opposition, to the altars found in Catholic churches. The church was an architectural symbol of the celestial community in which humanity participated and by which it was sustained. As such, churches were bulwarks that served a military function. In times of war, the Christian community huddled together inside the church with their sacred objects. In times of festivity or natural disasters, they sanctified the space in their villages by making processions outdoors with these objects.

The hierarchy of power that the Catholic Church ascribed to the sacred was visually represented on the ornamental altar screens, or *reredos*, that stood as

Ramón A. Gutiérrez

backdrops for the main altar in every church. These screens, physically attached to the altar on which the miracle of the Mass occurred, conjoined the community of the faithful with the communion of saints. The altar screen, divided horizontally into three ascending sections that rose up behind the altar, was an image of the heavenly order and a visual representation of salvation history. Reigning over the top was an image of the Trinity, portrayed either as three persons—God the Father, His Son, Jesus Christ, and the Holy Ghost—or as a triangular burst of light. The two *reredos* sections below this one were usually subdivided into various niches in which statues of Mary, the mother of Christ, of St. Joseph, Christ's foster father, and of the various virgins, martyrs, apostles, and angels were placed. When Christians stood before these altar screens and gazed at the persons represented there, they stood as participants in a long historical genealogy of the Catholic Church and could imagine their place in the celestial order.

Such were the official meanings of the altars and *reredos* that adorned every Catholic Church. But the construction and emplacement of altars was also an act of private devotion with ancient indigenous meanings. Despite the attempts of Christian clerics to eradicate such native practices in the initial years of the conquest, these practices persisted. At first they persisted clandestinely in the security of homes as acts of Indian contestation and opposition to the religion of their dominators. Secretly the Indians clung to their indigenous statues and icons. They continued to make covert offerings and to worship at sites that were holy in the preconquest topography.

As time passed and as the violent memories of the Spanish conquest faded, what developed in Mexico was a syncretic Christianity that creatively blended Christian theology and pre-Columbian animist beliefs. Around the sacraments and the official ritual of the Church a rather rigid orthodoxy prevailed. But if Christianity was to succeed, at least in its external manifestations, the Church fathers realized that they had to be flexible and adapt to the local terrain. This flexibility was eventually displayed in the elaboration of paraliturgies that were deeply significant to the Indians, through such things as didactic plays, rituals of planting, harvest, and first fruits, and rituals that venerated the souls of the dead. The space, time, and objects of the Christian cosmology were thus combined in complex ways with the space, objects, and time that Mexico's Indians had long observed. Mimicking and contesting, dissimulating and resisting, these have been the themes of Mexican Christianity over the last five hundred years. These are the themes that Dana Salvo's photographs of contemporary domestic altars in southern Mexico splendidly record.

Ramón A. Gutiérrez

Twice during the course of the religious year, during the week-long celebrations that commemorate the Day of the Dead at the end of October and the first days of November, and again at the conjunction of Christmas and the winter solstice, domestic altars become sites for much more elaborate celebrations. In Dana Salvo's photographs of home altars during the *Día de los Muertos*, or the Day of the Dead, one sees the syncretic mixing that developed in Mexican Christianity. Christian icons and statues and even the concept of the soul are brought together and combined with much older indigenous animistic beliefs about the ways in which the spirits that inhabit every living thing are connected and animate the universe.

On the very day that we celebrate the pagan residue of Halloween in the United States, Mexicans begin their week-long commemoration of their ancestral dead by constructing elaborate home altars, or by embellishing even further those altars that already occupy the home. Everything placed on these altars is there to entice the absent spirits of the dead to visit their living brethren. Bear in mind that throughout Mexico these celebrations on the *Día de los Muertos* take very different forms. In modern urban centers, in places like Mexico City and Guadalajara, skeletons and sugar skulls, which are pre-Columbian representations of the spirits of the dead, are combined with a repertoire of figures taken from television and popular culture: Batman, Dracula, demons, and ghosts. In some locales the elaborate celebrations staged to create a communion with the dead occur on altars constructed at cemeteries. The festivities Dana Salvo has photographed occurred in the home.

The home altars constructed on the Day of the Dead are most easily identified by the marigold flowers or *zempoalxochitl* (a Nahuatl word meaning "flower of the dead"), that adorn them. Since time immemorial the Indians of Mexico have cultivated marigolds as part of the offerings that are presented to the spirits of the dead. It is believed that the rich and sweet fragrance of marigolds attracts the spirits to the altar on which they are remembered and on which offerings have been set out to nourish them. Sometimes marigold petals are arranged in a pathway to and from the cemetery to assure that souls do not lose their way either to or from the feast, and thereby wreak havoc. And lest there be any confusion among souls as to what day is being celebrated, the intense blue smoke of copal incense shows them the way, a smell that the Indians of Mexico regard as the super odor of the center of the earth.

The altars constructed for the dead do not differ much from the domestic altars that families maintain year around. But on the Day of the Dead, pictures and items that belonged to their dearly departed are featured more prominently on the altar, along with the images of the Christian spirits, or saints. What does characterize the decorations and offerings that are placed on the domestic altar on this day are foods of various sorts. These foods vary enormously if the devotional practice occurs in an Indian village or a mestizo town. On altars constructed by Indians one often finds corn, squash, beans, bananas, and baked bread figurines, along with copal incense, candles, flowers, and tissue paper banners on which the spirits of animals are represented. On altars constructed by mestizos, these same elements are present, but in addition, bottles of soft drinks, Christmas decorative lights, and occasionally patriotic symbols such as flags and political posters also appear. Whatever the combination, the desired result is the same. The souls of the dearly departed visit the altar that has been set out for them, nourish themselves with their living relatives on the food that has been set out for this common union. And a communion it is indeed, for by the living and dead uniting on this day, by sustaining themselves on the nourishment that the earth produces, society is renewed and regenerated so that it may peacefully continue.

Ramón A. Gutiérrez

47

The third ritual moment that Dana Salvo records in his photographs are the celebrations during the Christian feast of Christmas, or what Mexicans have long marked through winter solstice rituals, that again take domestic altars as one of their major focal points. Like the altars constructed for the Day of the Dead, the *nacimientos* or nativity scenes that adorn home altars at the end of December and beginning of the new year are sites of artistic creation and are physical spaces where the complex history of the interaction between pre-Columbian indigenous beliefs and Christianity are brought together in symbolic whole. Like a family photo album filled with memories of the past, memories from the realm of organized Christianity, and memories of a deeper ancestral past, the home altar gives them a tangible and visual quality. The world of these memories, the world of private devotion in a part of Mexico far removed from our own, is the world that Dana Salvo opens here for us in his stunning photographs.

Conjuring the Holy

memorial &
devotional
altars

23. A shrine to Santa Rosa has a TV antenna standing cross-like beside the table. Strung balls hang from the ceiling against a shiny blue plastic backdrop, Chiapas.

24. A cross stands solidly behind a bowl of seeds, and saintly images are placed alongside old family photos, Chiapas.

25. Alpida and Jose Antonio Abadia
Nijenda keep this shrine devoted to
their ancestors and family, Chiapas.

26. A home in Chiapa de Corzo. An icon is holding the Christ Child with hand-cut paper flowers surrounding the table covered with plastic stars. A plastic bag holds an ancestral portrait. The stained wall on the left indicates the introduction of running water.

27. A chair transformed
into an altar, Campeche.

28. A household shrine with an icon box, holy cards, and family photographs. The looms and trestles are for Fausto Torrez's elaborate fishing nets.

29. This shrine is in the home of Fausto Torrez, outside Ticul, Yucatán. His home is also a small shop selling books and assorted items.

30. Nuestra Señora de Guadalupe has a place of honor among family photographs in this home, Yucatán.

31. Mrs. Santiago sits in her bedroom, beneath a pink canopy. Alongside the bed is a table devoted to her faith, Chiapas.

32. A widow's altar in Chiapas in memory of her husband. An older woman in the town, she had been the keeper of the painted backdrops for many years because a fire damaged the church.

33. This assemblage is referred
to as the Memory Wall, with
photographs of departed
family members, Chiapas.

34. *Ofrenda* with marigold-covered *arco*, sugar skulls and animals, and bread for the dead, Janitzio, Michoacán.

FLOWERS AND SUGAR SKULLS FOR THE SPIRITS OF THE DEAD

Salvatore Scalora

El *Día de los Muertos* is the homecoming of the spirits of the dead all over Mexico, a reunion of the dead and the living. The old ones say that when the spirits come back to the world of the living, their path must be made clear, the roadway must not be slippery with the wet flood of human tears. It is only in Mexico that death is the occasion of a vast annual celebration. Though death is feared, it is embraced without denial and even becomes the subject of humor. Coinciding on November 1 and 2 with the Catholic holy days of All Saints' and All Souls' known as *Todos Santos,* the Day of the Dead is the most important religious observance of the year. Preparations begin months ahead of time, and as the weeks draw nearer, activity in the marketplaces swells as the artifacts and foodstuffs known to please the dead are consumed by the living, thus feeding the economy as well.

In the Mexican psyche, there is no greater duty than to commemorate the family dead. This tradition has its roots back to the time of the Aztec civilization, ingrained with beliefs in a mystical universe, where death was viewed, not as the end of existence, but as a gateway to other levels. The eternal cosmic turbine spun with the cyclical energy of life and death, lubricated with sacrificial blood. During the time of the conquest, these pre-Columbian precepts merged with the Christian canon of the eternal existence of the soul after death in Heaven, Purgatory, or Hell. The modern-day celebration of the Day of the Dead survives as one of the most glorious fruits of the postcolonial religious garden—a hybrid of the Roman Catholic sacred and the indigenous.

The conquering culture, based on Spanish traditions, cast its mantle over the native people. The mestizo religious culture that evolved was a reconstruction of both belief systems. This slowly evolved synthesis modified both; some rites and practices disappeared and others emerged. The formal enactment of modern Roman Catholic practices celebrating *Todos Santos* is an example of the substantial merging of two vibrant religious cults. The poetic words of noted Mexican painter, engraver, editor, stage designer, teacher, and cultural promoter Gabriel Fernández Ledesma, describe this synergistic emergence.

> According to popular feeling, the new gods have not completely displaced the old. . . . In the ritual of the cult of ancestors, breads and sweets forming part of the offering represent figures of pagan myths and mix the symbols of their traditional religion with those of the Catholic cult. From one or another they take that which calms their desperation, which exalts their fantasy, and which fits—in the most comfortable manner—their poetic feeling and their plastic preferences.

Flowers and Sugar Skulls

In the Aztec cosmology, life springs from death, which is the raw material of life. Life and death are co-dependent. For the Aztecs it could be better stated that death fed upon life. Death allowed for the spilling of sacrificial blood and for offerings of beating hearts to the gods. These were the Aztec's payment of tribute, so that the sun would move across the sky and the maize would grow and feed the people.

The Aztecs ritualized the passage of death with specific rites. The dead were customarily buried with their clothes, food, and items of value to assist the souls with the afterlife journey. This passage was very long and challenging. Death was no easy escape; the comforts of the afterlife must be earned. Sometimes the souls lingered on earth for a time before they began their spiritual migration. The Aztecs believed that it took four years to complete successfully the task of traveling to the realms of the dead. This period of time was marked with specific funerary rites by the living. The dead were provided elaborate ceremonies in the calendar year to honor their souls' progress. The "Little Feast of the Dead" and the "Great Feast of the Dead" commemorated dead children and adults respectively. At these times dancing and singing were combined with offerings of chocolate, foodstuffs, drinks, and candles to the dead.

During the colonial period, the Catholic Church transferred these pre-Hispanic celebrations to the observance of *Todos Santos*. Many of the Church's beliefs in afterlife were easily assimilated into Indian beliefs. The common ground between Aztec and Christian beliefs was the recognition that dying was part of a cycle into another level of existence. According to Roman

Salvatore Scalora

Catholic tradition, as stated in the New Catholic Encyclopedia, the Feast of All Saints' was a commemoration of all the Christian saints and all the known and unknown martyrs. All Souls' Day commemorated the faithful departed. Requiem masses were celebrated for all the souls in Purgatory to help them attain the final cleansing and purification of their sins, so that they may finally ascend to the Kingdom of Heaven and be admitted to the Beatific Vision. Celebrants recited prayers in memory of the dead, with special intentions for one's own deceased family members. These prayers were but one of the traditions of this holiday; others included the parish procession to the graveyard, visiting the graves of relatives and friends and bringing gifts of fresh flowers, and lighting candles to the dead. This rich blend of Christian religious observances with their fulfillment of familial reconnection has sustained the celebration of *Día de los Muertos*.

Popular imagery related to the Day of the Dead focuses on skeletons and devils. The representation of death through the use of skeletal imagery is universal. Devil imagery is associated with the holiday because of the Catholic Church's admonition to lead a saintly life or be banished to Hell or Purgatory. In the devils' imaginary kingdom, skeletons and devils dance together, devils ride wild skeleton horses, devils push their sweethearts on tree swings, and they also ascend into the sky while riding in helium balloon gondolas.

Much of the celebration is invisible to outsiders who visit Mexico at the time of the Day of the Dead. While their tourist eyes will focus on the displays of colorful artifacts that surface throughout the mercados, hotel lobbies, museums, bakeries, and even airport concourses, the true essence of the holiday

Flowers and Sugar Skulls

observance is the ritualized and private practice of traditions that are sacred. *Norteamericanos* are tolerated at public aspects of the holy days, but the traditional Indian people rarely allow them into their humble homes. They are fiercely proud, organized into tribal groups with ancient-sounding names such as Zapotec, Mixtec, Chamulan, Tzotzil, Purépecha, Totonac, and Otomi. The obvious surface expressions of the Day of the Dead hold little visual clue as to how the artifacts function culturally or how they are integrated into the process of receiving the dead back on earth. The outsider must begin any study of this profound ritual by acknowledging that the Indian cultures surviving in Mexico today, by various degrees, continue to live with one foot planted in the world of their ancestors, a world infused with mystery and spirituality.

Salvatore Scalora

Dana Salvo, his artist wife Dawn Southworth, and their daughters, Jahna and Simone, observed the Indian customs during their numerous trips to Mexico. Traveling to tiny villages in the areas of Chiapas, Oaxaca, Yucatán, and Michoacán, Dana Salvo and his family were, over a period of time, warmly received into the homes and hearts of the native people. It was precisely because Salvo traveled with his family that the usual cultural barriers were lifted. The children, especially, endeared themselves to everyone around them. Thus, familial curiosity turned to conversations that ultimately led to invitations to visit native homes.

Salvo made photographs of home altars during the Christmas, Easter, and Day of the Dead holidays. His study of the altars of the dead took him to the state of Michoacán, to the bustling lake-side town of Pátzcuaro, to Tzintzuntzan, ancient capital of the Purépechas (called the "Tarascans" by the invading Spanish), and to Janitzio Island populated by 1,500 Purépecha descendants. Janitzio is a tiny glimmer in the brownish green waters of the crescent-shaped Lake Pátzcuaro. The island is a rough mound, topped by a surreal, oversized stone statue of the patriot-priest José María Morelos, the father of the Mexican constitution.

There, inside the crude homes and earthy huts he visited, Salvo saw wonderful altars. He encountered magic in its natural state. Spectacularly beautiful and spiritually blessed, these altars were arranged from simple materials by humble people. In order to record these temporal constructions, Salvo brought with him photographic equipment that, to his hosts, was the equivalent of magic: flashing strobe lights and a 4×5 wooden view camera mounted on a tripod, armed with a cyclopian glass eye-lens. He began his picture-taking sessions by shooting exploratory images using a Polaroid back to assess composition and quality of light. Working beneath his camera's black cloth further enhanced Salvo's own ritualized picture-taking ceremonies. In turn, he was able to share this process with his hosts. When they held these Polaroids between their fingers, they were able to touch and gaze at the magic, shimmering images. These photos became treasured objects that were often given a place of honor on the altar itself. Returning over a period of several years to the same homes, Salvo and his family were able to continue friendships and document the inevitable changes of *ofrendas* over the years. His visits were clearly part of a serious study, and his hosts were assured that he was not a "stealer of souls." This reassurance was of some notable comfort to people

Flowers and Sugar Skulls

who essentially still live by the spirit and are not afraid to commune with the spirits of their dead who may assist with the affairs of the living.

Photographs are in fact cherished in native cultures. On the Day of the Dead, throughout Mexico, photographs of the honored dead are placed upon the home altar, providing both a spiritual presence and memory triggers for family members and friends. The framed photographs are stand-ins for the dearly departed. Whether of newborn or aged, the portraits of the dead peer out at the living. Their presence is further enhanced by their inevitable proximity to holy pictures, chromolithographs of popular religious figures such as the Virgin of Guadalupe, the Holy Trinity, Christ on the Cross, and the saints and angels. This juxtaposition makes clear the exalted position within the spiritual realm to which the souls of the dead may lay claim. Just as the Catholic saints are thought to be intermediaries between the common people and the Holy Family, similarly the souls of the dead are beseeched to intercede favorably in the affairs of the living.

In Dana Salvo's Day of the Dead home altar photographs, shot on Janitzio Island (although a few were shot in Tzintzuntzan), we find very few family portraits of the dead placed alongside their extensive displays of holy pictures. Because of the poverty of their lives, photographs are a luxury to which they are unaccustomed. Here on Janitzio the dead are remembered, reimagined in the memory of the heart. Their names are whispered softly in prayers.

Throughout Mexico and beyond, the observances for the dead on Janitzio are considered among the most beautiful cemetery customs. The natural beauty of the island and her people is not to be confused with some notion

Salvatore Scalora

of artificially manicured beauty. The Purépechas live simply, their brick and cement houses nestle into the hillsides of rugged stone and crusty earth. They are resigned to the blessing and curse that tourism has brought to their home. Arriving on Janitzio, the tourists cart away plastic bags full of souvenir cups and mugs, sweaters and blankets, toy boats and fishing nets. Their stomachs fill up with the delights of Janitzio's dozen or so open-air restaurants. Especially during the Day of the Dead festivities, Janitzio can barely accommodate the swell of visitors.

Traditionally, on the day before the celebration, the butterfly-net fishermen ply the lake's waters on a duck hunt, armed with tri-pronged, wooden spears. Although the duck population appears to be dwindling, some still fall prey to the spear. These ducks are then plucked and cooked as a special offering laid on the home altar. On other days, the butterfly-net fishermen of the island pose for tourists arriving on the ferry launches. Their ancient-style nets are now supplanted by more traditional casting nets that are weighted down by small stones. The fishermen seek the delicately flavored *pescado blanco, trucha, charales,* and *boquerones* that live in the murky waters. Though locals lament that *Lago de Pátzcuaro* is drying up and becoming more polluted each year, it hasn't diminished their appetite for the shrinking fish harvest.

These hunting and fishing scenes alone help cast Janitzio in an ancient air, where traditions stand fast. However, there have been some cultural incursions from North America; relatives living in the southern U.S. have brought home to Mexico the Celtic-based celebration of Halloween. In Pátzcuaro's marketplaces, plastic jack-o'-lanterns and children's face masks are sold. In the main

Flowers and Sugar Skulls

Plaza Vasco de Quiroga, one will find confectionery black witches and orange jack-o'-lanterns among the sugar vendors' stalls which line one end of the square.

Recently, a new custom has been observed among children. It may be spurred on in part by the abundant presence of *Norteamericano* tourists. Several nights prior to the *Noche de Muertos,* the main plaza and the adjacent Plaza Bocanegrà and their connecting streets are filled with young children, carrying carved pumpkins with candles glowing inside, shouting, *"Calaverita! Calaverita!"* There they patiently await the hoped for dropping of coins into the jack-o'-lantern heads so that their families may offset the cost of flowers, bread, and sugar skulls for the dead. If you ask someone on the street if the American tradition of *Feliz Halloween* is taking over, you will hear a resounding, "No! We must resist. If we lose our roots, we die!"

The custom on Janitzio is to receive the souls of the dead children—*los angelitos*—on the evening of October 31 and the adults—*los difuntos*—on the evening of November 1. The children's spirits are first feted in the homes. It is customary to visit from house to house after dusk, bring presents for the dead, and recite prayers at the home altars. This is followed on November 1, *el Día de los Niños,* with visits to the cemetery for the placement of food, flowers, and candles during the morning vigil, *la velación de los angelitos,* which lasts from 6:00 to 9:00 in the morning. The entire household helps prepare the *ofrenda* by purchasing the necessary items, usually in Pátzcuaro, that must be a part of it, as well as preparing the various foods and drinks that will serve to satisfy the hunger and quench the thirst of the dead. Foods that were the favorites of the

Salvatore Scalora

71

honored dead are the requisite. The adults will be received during an all-night vigil at the cemetery for the *Noche de los Muertos* which lasts from midnight until 7:00 A.M.

On October 30, mothers and daughters prepare a special dough for the ceremonial *pan de muertos* — the bread of the dead. These small breads are baked into fanciful human and animal shapes and are used on the home altars, placed on the graves, and given as household offerings when visiting family and friends. Dana Salvo's image of women baking *pan de muertos* reveals the close connection among related family groups and the harmony of four generations of women working together. Meanwhile the men and young boys prepare the wooden stick trellises known as *arcos*, which are first covered completely with the traditional flowers of the dead — the *cempasúchil* or yellow marigolds. Using fishing line, the heads and short stems are wrapped tightly. Next, each *arco* is lavishly adorned with string-tied fruits such as oranges, apples, and bananas, a cosmic reverie of suns, planets, and moons. Fanciful creatures and spirits made of *pan de muertos* float among this fruitful universe. Finally, the sugar skulls and various other hollow white sugar candies are hung to complete the *arco*. The variety of these decorated candies runs a wide cultural and popular gamut: angels, dogs, cats, elephants, hens, beer and Coca-Cola bottles, babies, boots, sneakers, brides and grooms, and rabbits and turtles, among others.

The image of the *ofrenda* with bread (Plate 34) is a unique view of a tall arched *ofrenda* trellis, mounted on the altar table. In front of the plain trellis are two smaller but heavily decorated *arcos* which are built on tripod legs, like an

Flowers and Sugar Skulls

easel. We can observe the concrete blocks that keep the front legs from sliding forward. The smaller arches are made to be carefully transported to the gravesites and then transported back home to be part of the home altar. In these smaller arches we can see the profuse, decorative use of sugar candies; there are two sugar skulls at the top of each arch and a large number of dog-shaped confections. Mexicans view dogs as faithful companions, good company, and guides for the dead. Chronicler Fray Bernardino de Sahagún, a Franciscan friar who came to New Spain shortly after the period of the conquest, uncovered an interesting Aztec belief surrounding dogs and the afterlife journey of the souls of the dead. As the soul wandered through the descending levels of the netherworld, it eventually came to a great, wide river which had to be crossed. The soul met with dogs on the banks of the river to help it across. It was stated that yellow and black dogs were the guides.

This image also reveals the symbolic placement of the foods on the marigold-covered *arcos*. The arch shape is an ancient form representing both the resting bed board of the dead and the celestial dome of the heavens. Food is strung suspended from the arch to represent the bounty of the heavens. Several strings of flower heads, spaced apart, suspended to represent a rain of beauty and color from the heavens, specifically delineate the edges of the altar space, marking it as sacred space reserved for the dead. The completed *arco* gives homage to the bounty of life and symbolizes a cyclical system of life and death. Though designed for the pleasure of the souls of the dead, these symbolic structures reaffirm the thanksgiving of the living to God.

The *ofrenda* trellis with the dressed angel statue placed on a chair (Plate 35)

Salvatore Scalora

is endowed with an ecclesiastical reverence as well as a tenderness of loss. We are presented with a beautiful cosmic display with oranges as suns, bananas as crescent moons, and apples as planets. This universe is populated by fanciful Day of the Dead creatures in the form of sweetbreads. Behind the trellis, we can see the altar table and the death meal. It is believed that the spirits of the dead will consume the spirit—the essence, the vapors of the food offered them. The living will consume the remaining physical part, all in good time.

Salvo's image of the altar trellis with hanging red maize is another wonderful variation on the universe of bounty. Maize is the ancient food of the Aztecs, a sacred plant that ensured the continuation of life, the essential tribute to the gods. Below the trellis, on the small table, we observe the plates of food prepared especially for the dead. The altar table, set kitty-corner under the protective canopy of the colored tissue *papeles picados,* seems embraced by the holy chromolithographs attached to the upper walls. In the upper right, the beautiful heart-encrusted, suffering Madonna, the Mater Dolorosa, looks over the *arco.*

Appearing on many altars are casseroles of rice, plates of beans, enchiladas, tamales, tejocote fruits in syrup, tacos, tortillas, bread, fruits, bowls of candies and chocolate, and even pumpkin cooked with sugar. Drinks may include Coca-Cola, bottles of beer, tequila, and also *pulque* (native beer). Cigarettes are a special treat for deceased smokers, even if they may have died from a smoking-related illness. Tradition states that whatever items the household can afford should be purchased new: dishes, candle holders, incense burners, tablecloths, baskets, and so on.

The photograph of Pilar's *ofrenda* (Plate 40) is an especially beautiful table altar. We note the glasses of water for the soul's refreshment and spiritual cleansing. Water is believed to ward off evil spirits during the practice of funerary rites, spirits who may be interfering with the soul's safe journey to the netherworld. On the floor are pumpkins and other fall harvest crops. The chairs that face each other, empty, guardians of the souls, are poetic manifestations of the ancient belief that the spirits *do* return to earth. What a lovely table has been set for them within a magical garden space. Set within the cramped, utilitarian, everyday function of Pilar's home, the *ofrenda* almost becomes surreal, two realities existing in the same time and space. The rich colors and appetizing smells of freshly prepared plates of food entreat the spirits. Yes, dine with your family once again! You are not forgotten! Refresh your soul!

Another interesting observance is made by examining Pilar's *ofrenda* of another year (Plate 41). Here Pilar sits at the table dressed in her mestizo-styled dress trimmed with lace and fronted with a decorative apron piece in the Spanish style. This is a timeless portrait of a proud Purépecha woman. Sprinkled on the two empty chairs on the right of the table are marigold petals. Pilar has placed these petals as signs for the souls that their places are reserved for them. The custom of using marigold petals as signs and markers is well documented. In other parts of Mexico, some families are reported to have sprinkled marigold petal trails from the graves to the homes, if the distance was not too great, for the souls to follow.

In front of the trellises, we view typical Michoacán black-glazed candle holders and in the middle, sitting on a gray cement block, an *incensario* for the burning of copal incense. The resin and resinous bark of the copal trees (the

Salvatore Scalora

Burseraceae family) are the smoldering source of the blue, pungent, smoky plumes that both bless the altar and the foodstuffs, and drive away any evil spirits. The pure, whitish resin is the most expensive, whereas the bark or dark strains of resin are the cheapest. The tall wax tapers are intended for burning over a long period of time, and those blended from beeswax and paraffin are the finest. Also in demand are short candles poured in glasses and paper wrappers for the home altars. It is believed that the spirits warm their cold hands and bodies over the candle flames.

For the celebrating families, there is much binding pride in the fulfillment of family duty. This is a time to come together, to catch up on gossip and news. The most important admonition is to give respect as best as you can. Adults should also seize the opportunity to instill in their children the knowledge of traditions that were passed on to them. There are many tales told to children that speak to the mortal dangers of disrespecting the dead. The following tale, which is but one that I have heard, sets its moral teaching upon the disastrous result of laziness.

One day, a man who is to be away for the *Noche de Muertos* tells his wife to prepare a nice offering and altar for his deceased mother. The man departs believing that his wife will be faithful to his instructions. The wife, however, is lazy and prepares nothing for her deceased mother-in-law. When the husband returns to the village the next morning, he meets his mother's spirit crying by the gate of the cemetery. She tells her son that she was not welcomed to his house. Being

Flowers and Sugar Skulls

so hungry and cold, she was eagerly looking forward to the candles, food, and drink. Nothing had been set out, not even a cup of chocolate! The man was so upset to hear this, he asked the spirit what should he do? His mother's spirit tells him to say nothing of what he knows and instead he is to ask his wife to take her finest dress from her wooden chest to wear when they attend morning mass together. The husband arrived home and did as he was asked to do. His lazy, foolish wife readily agreed. Upon kneeling at her wooden chest to retrieve her dress, she died instantly of fright and fell to the floor. Her beautiful lace dress had turned into a mass of *calaveras* and bones!

Salvo's image of four generations (Plate 37) posing in front of the camera for a family portrait is a photographic *recuerdo* of the fiesta. They stand and sit within the sacred space of their *ofrenda*. They resemble the living religious tableaux that may be witnessed in the cemetery in Iguala, Guerrero. Their *arco* is notable for its central spine of sugar women holding baskets of lake fish; they assert their roles as cooks and providers. In this private family moment, the mothers and the future mothers share a foothold in the symbolic space of the returning *almas*, the souls. They appear to rest secure, ringed by the *cempasúchil*, the flowers of the dead, in the belief that the souls will be pleased by their preparations.

Dana Salvo's photographs capture and document the shrouded as well as

Salvatore Scalora

the readily apparent cultural patterns. They do so with great sensitivity and restraint. Salvo has shed the skin of the outsider; he has become a trusted, respected guest and witness in the homes of the native people. The fact that Salvo's photographic procedures are time consuming and involve substantial equipment only adds to the seriousness of his purpose in his subjects' eyes. Commemoration is not an act of pointing and shooting to the Purépecha.

Flowers and Sugar Skulls

As the hour approaches midnight on the evening of November 1, *la Noche de Muertos* (*Animecha Kejtzitakua* in the language of the Purépechas), the women and children of Janitzio begin their walk through the narrow alleyways that lead to the ancient cemetery for the all-night vigil. While the family men help them carry the *arcos*, drinks, baskets of food, flowers, candles, and incense burners to the cemetery, the Purépechas regard the vigil as an affair better suited to the women, the givers of birth. The men help set up the adornments and nourishments at the graves and may remain some hours before retiring to their homes, but the women hold the esteemed position in their tradition of caretaking the souls of the dead.

There is an old colonial church close by the cemetery which is devoted to San Jerónimo, the patron saint of Janitzio. On the main floor of the church a table is set *para los animas*. Heaped with mounds of marigolds, breads, and fruits, and lighted with dozens of candles, it is a banquet table for the dead under the watchful eyes of the neon-illuminated host, San Jerónimo. Bluish, odorous copal smoke tinges the atmosphere inside.

The entire cemetery, cut into the rocky terrain, bordering an ancient

Franciscan chapel on the far end, is aglow with thousands of candles. The simmering, wavering wicks cast their golden light over the otherwise gloomy somberness of the graves and tombs. Church bells toll in the darkness. The Purépecha women, seated on the ground, with blankets and shawls to cover their heads and shoulders, have prepared graveside beds for the children. With the illumination of all-night tapers set before the marigold-covered *arcos*, the world of the dead is made magical, the grotesque is wondrous. Into the hours toward dawn, the women kneel and sway, reciting the rosary and chanting in Purépechan. Laughter and prayers fill the space of the *Campo Santo*. When dawn's light arrives, the sun rises up with a gentle orange glow, slowly warming and reflecting off the steel gray waters of the lake. With quiet dignity, the children rise up, sleepy-eyed, to catch a glimpse of the last of the dying candle flames. At 7:00 A.M., as the men come to join their families at the graves, the island priest leads a general benediction with prayers for the souls. The vigil is ended. The *arcos* and food offerings are then returned to the homes where the families will later feast on the leftovers. As they eat these food offerings, they will recite prayers in the names of their family dead.

The longing of the dead for the living is reaffirmed during each vigil by peculiar signs and occurrences—the odd snuffing out of a candle, a strange shadow, an unusual swirl of the copal, the tipping over of a glass for no apparent reason, the sensation of touch upon the hair, a whispered voice.

"When you love them truly, the dead are never far from your heart," an elderly Purépechan said to me.

"I carry my deceased wife's memory in my heart each day and night. When

Salvatore Scalora

79

I die, my children and grandchildren will welcome us both once a year, to our homeplace on Janitzio. *No se puede vivir sin amar, amigo!*"

This essay is dedicated to the memory of Mexican folk artist, Pedro Linares, who passed in January of 1992 at the age of eighty-five at his home in Mexico City.

Flowers and Sugar Skulls

altars for
day of the
dead

These seven photographs were made on Janitzio, a small island village populated by Purépechan Indians, in Lake Pátzcuaro, high in the State of Michoacán. They were made on three occasions: during the *Día de los Muertos* celebrations in 1988, 1991, and 1992.

Arcos are constructed of wood and elaborately adorned with marigolds, specially baked bread for the dead, sugar skulls and animals, fruits, and corn. Elegant candlesticks and incense burners guide the souls of the deceased to tables set with offerings of ceremonial food, soup, and beverages.

35. A wooden angel stands before a geometrically shaped *ofrenda*, decorated with bananas and oranges, symbolizing the moon and sun. Bread loaves tied to the structure were baked in animal shapes to help guide souls in the spirit world.

36. A shelf (nicho) with saints and a blue cross.

37. Four generations of a Purépechan family.

38. *Ofrenda* with *arco* alongside a table set with soups and Cokes for returning spirits.

39. A table set with offerings.

40. Pilar's *ofrenda*, 1991.

41. Pilar Incarción with *ofrenda,* one year later.

42. A Christmas tree, paper chimney, traditional manger scene with Three Kings, and family photographs populate this Nativity arrangement.

HOME ALTARS

private reflections of public life

William H. Beezley

ome altars have formed a part of personal devotions in Europe, Africa, and North America since well before the encounter of these cultures in the wake of the Columbus voyage. At least dating to Roman times, families in the Mediterranean basin had home altars to the household gods, the lares. At least dating from the rise of the Bantus, western African peoples maintained domestic relics. At least dating to the Toltec peoples, families in the Mexican central valley had personal shrines to deities. On both sides of the Atlantic these home shrines gave a personal character to more formal, more austere, and often more bureaucratic, hierarchical religions. At the same time, home altars reflected the broader character of the general society.

After the cataclysmic cultural encounter between Spaniards, Aztecs, and west Africans in what today we know as Mexico, home altars took on additional features. The dominant Spaniards imposed their version of Roman Catholicism on American and African subordinates and slaves as the official, public, and visible religion. Personal religious practices in the home became more idiosyncratic and home altars more individualistic as a result of the arrival of Europeans and Africans and of the fusion of religious activities. As one might expect of any practice expressive of the individual character of Mexico after 1521, these altars contained (and continue to contain) elements that represent the ethnic (that is racial) and class (more properly caste until the late nineteenth century) divisions of the society.

Colonial Developments

Elite colonial families built substantial houses that included home chapels with elaborate and often expensive altars. In some instances, these families went beyond mere chapels by using religious art and icons throughout the rooms and halls, strategically placed thereby manipulating the viewer's perceptions through the purposeful relationships between images and space. For example, images re-created the stations of the cross whose mnemonics tell the passion of Christ, but also in more subtle ways as well individuals expressed personal feelings of devotion to one or another saint.[1]

Meanwhile the indigenous peoples continued their use of home altars, retaining pre-Columbian symbols and references. The items on the home altars formed a mixture, not a syncretic mosaic, of religions. Pre-Catholic use of flowers, colors, and tobacco offerings continued side by side with candles, saints, and crucifixes. Early in the colonial period, the church hierarchy concluded that home altars had become the preserve of the old heretical religions, and especially satanic practices. Therefore, church officials, led by Padre Juan de Acosta, promoted the use of music and dances as a public prelude to the mass to draw the indigenous peoples away from their home altars to the public religious centers and later to the newly constructed churches. These friars attempted to eliminate the creation of home altars because of what they believed were the residual, although attenuated, pre-Columbian symbols. Other friars, especially as the colonial years wore on, attempted to convert the centers of domestic worship to Christian images,[2] with the idea of bringing Catholicism into the home.

Meanwhile the home altars of colonial mestizos revealed their hybridity in syncretic cultural terms. Unlike the indigenous altars that had discrete, seemingly parallel, but separate pieces, these melded together revealing the emerging character of Mexican religion as something more and less than both Spanish Catholicism and the indigenous theology.

Little is currently known of the domestic life of blacks in colonial Mexico, beyond their presence in the large numbers in tropical agricultural zones where they served as field hands and in the large cities, especially the capital, where they worked as domestics. Yet from the activities of their fellows in the Caribbean we know they preserved elements of their previous culture, particularly in their life away from the masters. Moreover, black artisans who carved and created icons and other religious symbols incorporated their sense of divinity and of beauty in their work.

Besides their personal and private characteristics, the home altars also provide an opportunity for adding a creative touch to the religious experience. Each altar served as the site of interaction between the secular and the divine worlds, the place where humans and deities established, negotiated, and maintained their relationships. In particular, individuals worked to create a mutually

William H. Beezley

productive relationship, that is, "the verbal goal of prayer and the visual goal of image assembly at the altar."[3]

During the eighteenth century, the home altars of the elite became known as *oratorios*, implying a larger, officially sanctioned site. These periodically caused a problem for local officials, who disputed the way in which people used them. Often elite families held dances before the altars or incorporated meals featuring cakes and hot chocolate (the holy beverage of the Aztec nobility) in the *oratorio*. These occasions, usually dedicated to a particular saint, often featured a young man, wearing the religious garments, in what the church hierarchy found to be a mockery of local priests. These affairs, especially if held by upwardly mobile mestizos, annoyed more proper elites, who regularly complained about this activity to inquisitional officials. The *criollo* judges of the Holy Office of the Inquisitors investigated and attempted to prevent such activities by suggesting the prohibition of private chapels with their family altars.[4] At precisely the same moment, the economic success of individuals in the eighteenth century resulted in a dramatic increase in the applications to church authorities for the blessing of altars in private homes.

Appearing first in the homes of the elite, but quickly spreading to the residences of all classes was a seasonal family altar called *nacimientos*, or manger scenes. This practice seems to date to 1223 in Italy when St. Francis of Assisi created a Nativity scene with live animals. The custom moved from Italy to Spain in the seventeenth century where these "Bethlehems" or *Belenes* exhibits appeared not only in churches and convents, but in the homes of the Spanish nobles as well. Spaniards brought the custom to Mexico by the eighteenth century, and soon households that could afford it had their own *nacimientos* during the Christmas season.

These home altars at first featured only the holy family of Joseph, Mary, Jesus. Carved wood, wax, and plaster representatives of the holy family quickly appeared and were soon followed by figures that had been overlaid with gold or silver and dressed in silk and other fine materials. Imported icons become the rage in Mexico City, with ivory figures brought from China and Philippines, porcelain ones from Italy, and specially painted ones from Guatemala. The highest praise for domestically produced replicas went to the figures made of silver from the Guanajuato and Zacatecas mining districts. The figures in the *nacimiento* expanded to include the wise men, shepherds, angels, and, in a particular Mexican addition, devils, who were grouped around the manger. The entire shrine often becomes quite valuable. For example, the inventory of goods at the death of the Countess of Xala in 1787 listed seventeen figures of the Magi, each with an entourage, six princes in specially made garments worked with silver ornaments, twelve shepherdesses and eighteen shepherds, an angel, Indians, thirty-four mules, sixteen cows, an ox, and a mule. Somewhat out of place in the scene were an old man leading a horse, thirty-six small animals, a hut with an old woman feeding her chickens, a small house, and a grove of trees. This Christmas altar had an assessed value of $1,077, a fortune in the eighteenth century.[5]

The second half of the 1700s witnessed the rise of Enlightenment ideals, Bourbon political reforms, and the Mexican local pride that climaxed in the wars of independence (1810–21) and in efforts to restrict the Roman Catholic

William H. Beezley

Church in Mexico. In the confusion of ideology, politics, and reform campaigns, the stricter regulations of the religious presence in civic society (for example, the expulsion of the Jesuits from Spanish possessions in 1867) resulted in the strengthening of neighborhood and individual religious practices.[6]

The Nineteenth Century

Home altars grew in importance, it appears, as secularization advanced during the nineteenth century. Those in urban areas certainly gained more significance as city councils began ordering that holy images in public niches outside buildings be moved inside to avoid disrespect from a population stepping away from church-dominated public space. This new urban legislation reflected efforts to make public life more secular by ending in this way the customs that required some show of reverence, such as kneeling or pausing to make the sign of the cross before icons, a tradition increasingly honored in the breach. The new laws also resulted from a realistic desire on the part of the local authorities to avoid attempting to enforce unenforceable traditions. At the same time, these authorities did not want to permit any seeming irreverence to holy images. The solution, many government officials believed, was to move the holy images inside churches and other buildings, including homes.[7]

These quite reasonable adjustments to public life in the early years after independence reinforced the custom of home altars. The importance of these private and personal shrines received further significance during the years of religious turmoil (1854–67), especially during the civil war over the separation

Home Altars

of church and state (1858–61). In some regions of Mexico, the tradition of home altars continued the seasonal significance, through the practice of women preparing special home altars during the Day of the Dead, Christmas, and Easter celebrations. Certainly in some areas such as Oaxaca and Tlaxcala, this practice drew on much earlier indigenous customs.[8]

The importance of home altars grew after independence and before the 1890s because of the church-state conflicts associated with the rise first of federalist and then of liberal politics, that climaxed in the wars of the Reform era (1858–61) and the French intervention (1862–67) and the strident anticlerical politics led by Benito Juárez during the same years. The result was the decline in Mexico of the number of both priests and temples from 1821 to 1880. There was a concomitant retreat of the churchmen from several areas, so that much of rural Mexico received visits by circuit-riding priests as seldom as once a year or even less frequently. Religion was left more and more during the nineteenth century in the hands of the laity. Family-based religious practice centered around the home altar became the norm. The mid-century wars of the Reform, which particularly aimed at secularizing all aspects of public life, contributed to the private character of Mexican Catholicism, with Mexicans focusing on their own household shrines.

During these years of the nineteenth century, as the public influence of the Roman Catholic Church waned, leaving home altars the centers of popular religion, the Virgin of Guadalupe emerged not only as the popular symbol of Catholicism but also as the most prevalent emblem of Mexican nationalism. Thus the iconography that incorporated her image in home altars also

William H. Beezley

indicated homage to the nation, even though for most of the first eight decades the country was largely in shambles.

During the 1890s, Mexico underwent a new wave of evangelization that resulted from the return of newly trained, eager priests from the Colegio Pio-LatinoAmericano in Rome and from the encouragement offered by the papal doctrine expressed in *Rerum Novarum*. Thus, enthusiastic priests prompted by the social ideals of the new papal concerns for social action over church doctrine soon resulted in an increased number of churches, of priests, and of attendance at formal services after 1895. The marker of these developments was the formal crowning of the Virgin of Guadalupe, October 12, 1895. The result of this campaign was to invigorate religious activity and to strengthen the daily practice of religion that in turn prompted increased attention to the family's home shrine.

The reinvigoration of the formal church did not detract from the role of domestic shrines. The home altars, intended as a threshold to the divine, also serve as a collection of the tastes, habits, and interests of everyday Mexicans. The collage of religious icons, especially lithographs of favorite saints and prayer cards are mixed in a deliberate arrangement by the owner. With the nineteenth-century perfection of both printing and lithography, these centavo images and chapbooks became increasingly common. In the 1890s, anthropologist Frederick Starr collected these prayer sheets, called *alabanzas*, each with a devotion to the saint or Virgin pictured on the card. Antonio Vanegas Arroyo printed the prayer sheets and sold them for five centavos. A few examples even have bilingual prayers, with both Spanish and Nahua, the language of the Aztecs, versions of praise to the religion icon.[9]

Twentieth Century

Technological, commercial, and political changes in the twentieth century contributed to changes in the home altars. For example, the altars done during the Days of the Dead began to incorporate pictures of departed relatives as the technology of photography improved, the price of photos declined, and the equipment became more common.[10] These photographs gave an even greater human character to the altars that also featured other items of departed relatives, such as their favorite drinks and meals, cigarettes, and personal items. Pictures of relatives and lithographs of the Virgin and the saints create a relationship between the holy and the altar-makers' families, establishing connections by the placement of the icons and images. Moreover, by placing *milagros* (the tiny representations of human limbs and animals to represent divine cures of injuries, relief of pain, and the recovery of lost pets) on the altar, the story of the family's encounters with adversity and illness are told through a kind of pictograph that ends by stating the efficacy of prayer.[11] The location of the *milagros* near the Virgin or the image of a favorite saint provides a tribute to the helpfulness of that divine personage. All the personal altars in this way offer a snapshot of everyday life in Mexico that is impossible to capture in other ways.

These contemporary home altars share motifs with Mexico's formal artistic heritage that merges a variety of forms with vestiges of the pre-Columbian

William H. Beezley

heritages.[12] Perhaps nowhere is that overlap made clearer than in the use of flowers and foods. The use of food also makes clear the relationship between the altar and the table—the first Christian altar being the table used for the Last Supper. Thus, food and flower arrangements offer a visible reminder of this relationship. Moreover, the actual items serve as statements that the viewers can understand. The most common material metaphor, for example, is the rose, the symbol of the Virgin of Guadalupe. Other common items include the egg-yolk bread to feed the souls of the departed during Day of the Dead. Thus a lexicon of items generally known, but also with family-specific meanings, exists.

Contemporary home altars can be divided into two general categories: everyday altars and seasonal shrines. The first group is most expressive of the owners' interests, such as a favorite saint, a favorite appearance of the Virgin, a favorite prayer and favorite devotion that include candles or prayer sheets or rosary beads. Here it is necessary to remember that these items all have specific and individual meanings and memories, and together they have multiple and multilayered significance. Where, when, and by whom they were obtained create a story for each item and together a history of the altar that recalls individuals, journeys, pilgrimages, and fulfillment of promises to saints. In many cases they represent a visible memory of a miracle performed, a prayer answered, an illness cured, a danger averted, or a child protected. Each altar can be read as a family album that includes the family and its deities and an iconic portrait of negotiations between family members and the divine, in which requests and promises are traded; saints are praised or demoted (removed from the altar, for example) in exchange for favors or in disappointment at unfulfilled requests.

Each of these items recalls many religious and secular associations at the same time. As Victor Turner has written,

> celebratory objects are, first and foremost, material objects, though they represent ideas, objects, events, relationships, "truths" not immediately present to the observer, or even intangible or invisible thoughts and conceptions. Such celebratory symbols, moreover, usually stand for many things and thoughts at once.

William H. Beezley

He continues to say, "We are seldom dealing with separate symbols but with clusters made up of objects, actions, sounds, states, orders, contracts, each unit, act, or thing, at once itself and standing for more than itself, the ensemble making up more than the sum of its parts."[13]

The seasonal altars expand the personal altars with holiday items. Day of the Dead altars (mentioned above) have an individual character representing deceased relatives. They also have general characteristics associated with the holiday. Day of the Dead, for example, often requires sugar cane stalk and flower arches around the altar and marigold petal carpets as an approach from outside the front door leading to the altar. The altar also incorporates egg-yolk bread, bowls of mole, and cups of chocolate made with water rather than milk; these foods, specifically associated with this holiday, are served in new crockery each year. Somewhat comparable to the *nacimientos* of the Christmas season are the vignettes called "Los Padrecitos," the little Fathers—skeletal priests in a miniature funeral procession with a coffin. These "Padrecitos" are placed on the altar during the season.

The home altars for Day of the Dead have a compact, public analog in the graveside shrine for the same period. This home altar brings together the divine, the dead, and the living in an effort to create a model of good, productive relationships. It is especially important to lure the souls of the dead to the altar, so they are attracted by marigolds, candles, and favorite foods. Visitors also bring gifts that are placed on the altars to attract the *muertos*, the dead souls. As friends and family gather around this special home altar, it provides the opportunity for story-telling, especially reminiscences, and sharing holiday foods. The altar thus provides the site for strengthening the community of living persons, by recalling the dead and the divine through anecdotes.[14]

Similar activities surround the other common seasonal home altar, the *nacimiento*. The Navidad celebration uses a wider range of flowers than the Day of the Dead celebration, and, of course, typically a crèche. In the twentieth century, this manger scene, usually festooned with fresh flowers and Spanish moss, may become a part of the everyday altar as a devotion to the Christ Child. Whether or not it does, the manger scene takes on personal aspects as it grows from the holy family (called the *misterios*) and worshippers identified in the Bible to include family, local community, and occupation members. Small carved wooden, clay, wax, plaster, straw, or plastic figures of favorite animals and local artisans, such as taco and balloon vendors, are represented. Over the years, the manger scene becomes a visual family tree and historical record of the occupations, education, and friendship of the owner. It also blends together the worldly and divine in a way that makes visible the way that one person beholds the intersection of these worlds. Although virtually everything typical of local communities may be found in these home altars, they never include images of pigs—because of the popular wisdom that pigs did not live in the Holy Land during Biblical times. Nevertheless turkeys, electric trains, airplanes, Christmas trees, snow, and, of course, an array of automobiles and trucks appear in different family altars.[15]

A Mexico City *nacimiento,* described by Frederick Starr in 1930, was "built up on a table in the front room. The whole table is filled with it. It is covered with rocks and sand and moss built up to look like a hilly country. There are little trees and a narrow winding road. There are little houses and an inn and a stable. In the stable is the manger with a little figure of the Christ child and figures of Mary and Joseph. Little figures of cows and donkeys stand around."[16]

Contemporary manger scenes also have regional characteristics that reflect the ethnic and geographic diversity of Mexico. The towns of Celaya and Salamanca in the state of Guanajuato are known for their elaborate and beautifully constructed *nacimientos.* Metepec in the state of Mexico, famous among folk art collectors for its artisans who make the wonderfully elaborate trees of life, produces Christmas versions of this art form that work a nativity scene into the tree of life to place on the home altar.[17] In the far north and across the Rio Grande into south Texas, paper flowers form a crucial part of both seasonal and everyday altars. These *coronas para los muertos* or crepe paper flowers represent a folk art that continues today.[18]

William H. Beezley

Everyday home shrines serve as niches of popular interest, not just of divine intercession and the afterlife, but of everyday concerns, habits, interests, and pleasures. In this way, the altars reflect broader themes in Mexican life. The commercialization of Mexican society becomes clearly evident in the brand-name items included in the home altars of contemporary times. This is a result of the rise of the producer and consumer society that first began appearing after the expulsion of the French in 1867. Perhaps the most dramatic of all the industries in respect to advertising and marketing were the cigarette companies, and, of these, Buen Tono dominated the field from the 1880s through World War II when a variety of brands emerged and dominated the field.[19]

Nevertheless, it would be simplistic to see items such as cigarettes on the altar as only the successful creation of a consumer society by Mexican businesses. Cigarettes, for example, represent much more: clearly the package of smokes recalls the habits and preferences of a departed relative, undoubtedly re-creating his or her behavior, when the departed smoked, how the cigarette was lighted, and the smell of the tobacco and the smoker. The package also recalls traditions stretching back before the arrival of the Spanish to the use of tobacco as a ritual product that often had special effects on participants in different curing and prayer ceremonies.[20]

Moreover, it must be remembered that above all the maker of the altar is a folk artist, who captures visibly the vitality of religious beliefs, the family, and the community in the collage of items on the altar. Folklorist Kay F. Turner has adapted the aesthetic of Miriam Schapiro to identify this folk art as *femmage*, for the "process of collecting and creatively assembling odd or seemingly disparate elements into a functional, integrated whole piece." In home altars this process results in the assemblage of "a family of images that synthesizes and projects the fundamental social and spiritual values of the family: nurturance, relation, and a sense of place."[21]

All the vitality, individuality, and artistic character of everyday Mexicans appear in the home altars included in this volume. In the photographs that follow, Dana Salvo has captured both the artistic and ethnographic value of these shrines. Their significance is felt in each image—as the owners reached out to the deity, they reveal most clearly their humanity, and show the observer the interests of ordinary people dealing with their world through this folk art form.

William H. Beezley

Notes

1. See the excellent paper, Rosalva Loreto López, "La Fuerza de la Imagen en la Conformación de la Religiosidad familiar en la Puebla de Los Angeles en el siglo XVIII" (unpublished paper).

2. Richard C. Trexler, "We Think, They Act: Clerical Readings of Missionary Theatre in 16th Century New Spain," in Steven L. Kaplan, ed., *Understanding Popular Culture* (Berlin: Mouton Publishers, 1984), p. 195 and footnote 21, p. 219.

3. Kay F. Turner, "Mexican American Home Altars: Towards Their Interpretation," *Aztlan-International Journal of Chicano Studies Research* 13, nos. 1–2 (1982), pp. 323–24, esp. p. 312.

4. The Inquisition Records for the late colonial period contain extensive correspondence on the issue of family chapels and altars. Linda Curcio-Nagy provided this reference.

5. Corinne Ross, *Christmas in Mexico* (Lincolnwood, Ill.: Passport Books, 1976), pp. 17–19.

6. This is a speculative conclusion based on the prevalence and increased importance of barrio and village virgins, most dramatically demonstrated when Padre Miguel Hidalgo used the local banner of the Virgin of Guadalupe to lead the movement for independence, the appearance of messianic leaders to reinstate the church, and miracles performed by local saints during the wars of independence. Much

research on this topic remains to be done. For a start, see Guy Thomson, "Francisco Lucas," (unpublished manuscript) discussing the Puebla village of Zacapoaxtla, p. 380, footnote 101; José Luis Mirafuentes Galván, "Identidad india, legitimidad y emancipación política en el nororeste de México (Copala, 1771), in Jaime E. Rodríguez O., *Patterns of Contention in Mexican History* (Wilmington, Del.: SR Books, 1992), pp. 49–67; various articles by Eric Van Young, including "The Cuautla Lazarus: Double Subjectives in Reading Texts on Popular Collective Action," *Colonial Latin American Review* 2 (1993):3–26; and David A. Brading, "Tridentine Catholicism and Enlightened Despotism in Bourbon Mexico," *Journal of Latin America Studies* 15 (1983):1–22.

7. Anne Staples, *"Policia y Buen Gobierno:* Municipal Efforts to Regulate Public Behavior, 1821–1857," in William H. Beezley, Cheryl E. Martin, and William E. French, eds., *Rituals of Rule, Rituals of Resistance: Public Celebrations and Popular Culture in Mexico* (Wilmington, Del.: SR Books, 1994), pp. 115–26.

8. An excellent introduction to these special seasonal altars can be found in Yolanda Ramos Galicia, ed., *Dos ofrendas de Día de Muertos en el estado de Tlaxcala* (Mexico: Instituto nacional de Antropología e Historia, 1992) and *Las Tradiciones de Días de Muertos en Mexico* (Mexico: Dirección General de Culturas Populares, 1987).

9. Frederick Starr Papers, UCLA Library, Department of Special Collections, Collection 190, Box 1, folders "Prayer Sheets" and "Various Illustrations."

10. For the early history of photography in Mexico, an excellent starting place is Teresa Matabuena Peláez, *Algunos usos y conceptos de la fotografía durante el Porfiriato* (México: Universidad Iberoamericana, 1991).

11. See Marion Oettinger, Jr., *The Folk Art of Latin America: Visiones del Pueblo* (New York: Dutton Studio Books, 1992), p. 43, and his *Folk Treasures of Mexico: The Nelson A. Rockefeller Collection* (New York: Harry N. Abrams, 1990), pp. 70–71 for an introduction to milagros.

12. See María Auxiliadora Fernández, "The Representation of National Identity in Mexican Architecture: Two Case Studies (1680 and 1889)" (Ph.D. dissertation, Columbia University, 1993), pp. v–vi.

13. Victor Turner, ed., *Celebration: Studies in Festivity and Ritual* (Washington, D.C.: Smithsonian Institution Press, 1982), pp. 16, 20.

14. See Suzanne Katherine Seriff, "Laughing Death: A Critical Analysis of the Days of the Dead Celebration in Oaxaca, Mexico" (M.A. thesis, University of Texas, 1984), especially pp. 43–48.

15. Ibid.

16. Frederick Starr Collection, Department of Special Collections, University of Chicago Library, Box 19, Folder 7.

17. Corinne Ross, *Christmas in Mexico*, pp. 19–20.

18. Curtis Tunnell and Enrique Madrid, "Coronas para los Muertos: The Fine Art of Making Paper Flowers," in Joe S. Graham, ed., *Hecho en Tejas: Texas-Mexican Folk Arts and Crafts* (Denton: University of North Texas Press, 1991), pp. 131–45.

19. Steven B. Bunker, "'Consumers of Good Taste': Marketing Modernity in Northern Mexico, 1890–1910" (M.A. thesis, University of British Columbia, 1994) examines the inchoate consumer society in Monterrey and Chihuahua City, especially the tobacco industry.

20. For some discussion of the use of tobacco and altars on Peru's north coast, see Donald Joralemon, "Altar Symbolism in Peruvian Ritual Healing," *Journal of Latin American Lore* 11, no. 1 (1985): 3–29, especially p. 13.

21. Kay F. Turner, "Mexican American Home Altars," pp. 323–24.

William H. Beezley

nacimientos

43. A shrine in the home of Consuelo and Ricardo Rincón Mendoza was constructed to celebrate the holidays of Christmas followed by the Feast of San Sebastian on January 22, Chiapas.

44. Outside the city of Oaxaca, this *nacimiento,* with a large painted canvas with the Eye of God, is a gaily constructed manger scene. The empty basket in the center is awaiting the birth of Jesus.

45. This *nacimiento* was constructed with multiple babies Jesus for Christmas in the town of San Cristóbal de las Casas, Chiapas.

46. This young woman sits by her small *nacimiento* and Christmas tree. She created the five paintings
on the wall and around the manger scene. The portrait above her is of her mother, Yucatán.

47. Baby shoes hang above this Nativity scene with the Three Kings and Christ Child, Yucatán.

48. Manger scene
on a table, Yucatán.

49. A corner *nacimiento* with a manger scene sitting atop toys, and paper snowmen, Campeche.

50. An open hut in Yucatán with a Christmas altar in the corner.

51. A *nacimiento* with a purple canopy enclosing ferns and boughs. A golden sun shines down on Baby Jesus in a cradle.

52. The colors of the Mexican flag wrap around this altar honoring the patron saint
Nuestra Señora de Guadalupe. Coke bottles function as candle holders, Yucatán.

53. A traditional *nacimiento* constructed for Christmas. The old woman, the matriach of the family, is solely responsible for its creation, Chiapas.

54. This *nacimiento* is constructed of sewn burlap and canvas. In the center is the Santo Niño de Atocha, the patron saint of children.
Sitting alongside the *nacimiento* is the child Alicia. Her little plastic toy animals populate the manger scene, Chiapas.

AFTERWORD

Amalia Mesa-Bains

The world that Dana Salvo captures is a world of intricate and sincere spirituality. The context for understanding this world is culturally and historically illuminated in the essays by Ramón A. Gutiérrez, Salvatore Scalora, and William Beezley. Each brings an insight to the conditions and influences within the tradition of Mexican domestic altars. The specificities of the temporary and the permanent are distinguished by their insightful text. It is the aesthetic dimension within these specific forms that is of most interest to me. As a contemporary artist connected to the practice of domestic altars, I am deeply touched and inspired by Dana Salvo's capacity to seize the momentary. His delicacy is apparent in the lack of self-consciousness in the images. There is no sense of intrusion, even little sense of the act of mechanical reproduction. We forget that these two worlds of the ancient and the modern have met in the photographic event.

The ephemeral quality of the domestic altars known as *nacimientos* or Christmas crèches and the offerings to the dead are reflections of total commitment and faith in the momentary. Dana Salvo's photographs record what is essentially a fleeting gesture with substance, never sacrificing the power of the temporal. In his photographs of the *nacimientos,* Salvo establishes a dignity for the world in miniature that is brought into our view. The interplay of the real and the faux is never disturbing. *Papier-mâché* mountains and caves rest side by side with real greenery in the magic tableau of the crèche (Plates 53, 54). The artistic production of the *nacimientos* is based on a sincere decoration in which display and adornment have no limit, for they are a sign of the devotion of the family. Like creation myths they gain power commensurate with their complexity and richness. In the hands of another photographer they might be exposed to a harsh reality that would undermine their absolute simplicity. Salvo instead brings a gentle gaze to bear on the cherished site of the holy family, and we all share a trust in the promise of rebirth. A season of light is implicit in these *nacimientos* that seems to come from ancient rites of nature present long before Christianity. Materials are recycled in these creations that appear at first glance haphazard and accidental. It is upon reflection that the viewer recognizes an aesthetic logic to the practice of the everyday. The artist of the *nacimiento* must make do, yet even in the hardship and frugality of rural life we see a nobility of cultural production. What is saved throughout the year that has artistic and decorative value makes its way into the *nacimiento* in a fine balancing of theme and medium.

In this aesthetic of respect, the altar-maker remembers the dead in the creations of temporary offerings. We are drawn to Salvo's images as they take hold of the ephemeral nature of the offering or *ofrenda.* It is in the seasonal display of abundant foods and flowers that we understand the temporal qualities of both the *ofrenda* and the dead they honor. In this transitory reflection of Mesoamerican practices commemorating the dead, the artists, for that is what they are, call upon memory as the organizing device of expression. Like the seasons, the living and the dead are connected through this tradition of love and remembrance. Throughout the *ofrenda,* the artist makes use of aesthetic strategies to take the offering to its highest level of beauty. Abundance is often a measure of prosperity and regard for the dead, while it is also used to dazzle with accumulations of flowers, sugar objects, and elaborate *arcos* or flower-covered arches of bamboo. The special constructions for the Day of the Dead occupy or extend already existing permanent altars, which are the established spaces of the sacred in the home. These ephemeral offerings co-exist with the long-standing altars that record the family histories and prized possessions. Images of the sacred deities particular to regions and the aesthetic assemblage of objects and mementoes serve as the backdrop for occasional offerings to the departed souls. The altar cloths used include the everyday plastic as well as the hand embroidered, while candles and *papel picado* complete the traditional elements. It is Salvo's straightforward approach that registers these details with an honesty that is in keeping with the spirit of the offering.

The altars that are the continuous chronicle of the family faith and history are captured through the lens of the visitor. We are allowed to see the spare nature of the room, but its elegance is nonetheless transcendent. The sacred space is marked off by backdrops of popular materials such as patterned cloth, oil cloth, wrapping paper, and the selection of weathered walls. This minimalist aesthetic gives greater power to the central religious tableau, from plaster

Amalia Mesa-Bains

virgins and saints to colonial wood sculptures. There is an evident and conscious style of staging the spiritual activities. It is this sincere artistry that makes the images so compelling. For all their innocence, the altars are simultaneously examples of a directed artistic production. Detail and miniaturization also reflect both sacred and aesthetic concerns. The formal arrangements of space and color are set off by the seemingly haphazard accumulation of small objects and mementoes. Yet we sense that the interplay between objects is not just chance encounter of lived collecting, but a more focused preference for aesthetic combinations of the small and utilitarian. In this framing of the picture plane, Salvo gives us a vision of the artistic inventions at stake in the domestic altars. The cultural, regional, and historic influences are evident in the choice of materials and deities, but there is more that characterizes the practice of altar-making in the Mexican tradition. A number of strategies are consistent across the altars, including the use of canopies or ceiling treatments, which may be expressions of celestial imagery; the serialization of objects in formal arrangements; the emphasis on natural or aged surfaces which reflect a relationship with time and erosion; the balance between scale and volume; and the continuous presence of memorial materials.

In registering the aesthetic devices that the altar-maker employs we can never lose sight of the function of the altar. It stands as a spiritual and commemorative site that consolidates family histories narrated in the presence of mementoes from special events, as well as family photos. This chronicle is also a record of the power of nature in the spiritual world-view of indigenous peoples. In this capacity, the home altars can be seen as sites of resistance and redemption. Here signs of healing, the afterlife, and love are commingled in an overlapping phenomenon. In the home of the *curandero* we see one of the most elaborate and spectacular of the domestic altars reflecting a long accretion of experiences and memories. The archival quality is interwoven with a present-day sense of activity, where objects are used to bring the past to life. Extraordinary combinations of transcultural images and personal histories abound. Chinese dragons and serialized mourning cards intervene in the staging of the sacred. The *curandero* faces us within the backdrop of his own self-portraits and a complex array of images of the pope, a television set, *incensarios,* and empty Nescafe bottles that serve as vases for the floral offerings. Yet amidst this dizzying display of popular culture we find an almost melancholy sense of love and death, of lives gone and sorrow overcome in the sepia-toned archival family photos. The mixture of everyday objects and special sacred *regalia* all takes place within a conscious artistic vocabulary of the most contemporary nature. For me this photograph is the most persuasive and intriguing. The viewer enters a *mundo entero,* where all the moments are bound into one, past and present, public and private. Like the inseparability of the body and the mind, integral to *curanderismo* or the healing world-view, we experience the photograph as both a visceral and mythic place.

The photographs of Dana Salvo chronicle the unfolding and multiple worlds of spiritual belief that move between the signs of nature and its sacred origins and the mestizo symbolism of the Virgin of Guadalupe or ancient *Tonantzin* (Plates 22, 52). These images give us an insight to an indigenous world of the sacred rapidly disappearing through poverty and modernization. In this sense

Amalia Mesa-Bains

127

Salvo offers his own sacred space, the photograph. He seizes the fugitive expression in a time of precious cultural meaning. We are reminded of Walter Benjamin: "To articulate the past historically does not mean to recognize it the way it really was. It means to seize hold of a memory as it flashes up at a moment of danger."

Salvo has seized the memory through his images to give us an understanding of a way of life that is fast disappearing. He has transformed the private and spiritual space into one of public vision with respect, trust, and mutual artistry. We are grateful to glimpse the result of private processes that have known the joy of remembering the dead, where each day is lived with faith and the capacity to fashion beauty amidst poverty and struggle. Salvo has given us the narrative of the ancient and the new in his rare photographs.

a
curandero's
home

Plates 55–59 were made in the home of Don Filogonio Perez, a healer who lives in the mountains of Chiapas, in the town of San Ramón, outside San Cristóbal de las Casas. The photographs were made between 1987 and 1992. In addition to providing cures for a number of ailments, he is, among other things, a maskmaker, a storyteller, and an accomplished painter, as evidenced by the numerous paintings on his walls. He grows many of his herbs, as well as the calla lilies on his altar, in the courtyard outside his house. As depicted in the photographs, his home is an assemblage of objects and images which illustrate his strong faith and family history.

55. Don Filogonio Perez, 1992 .

56. Religious cards adorning a doorway.

57. A shelf and wall lined with assorted images, including a painted self-portrait, family snapshots, and a photograph of the Pope.

58. Snapshots of Don Filogonio's family life abound as well as a wide array of saints, along with numerous images
drawn from popular culture ranging from Nat King Cole (with a cross), to African tribal photographs.

59. An altar with a painting of a serpent, ceremonial masks, eggs, and the Christ Child, at Christmas.

Acknowledgments

I am sincerely grateful to those through whose hospitality, support, collaboration, friendship, and trust this book was made possible.

My family's life will forever be enriched by the many Mexican families who so generously opened their homes and hearts to us. The genuine affection extended to my wife, Dawn, and our children, Jahna and Simone, inspired our pilgrimage as we journeyed countless miles throughout Mexico this past decade. Words cannot adequately convey the depth of my gratitude. I wish expressly to thank Pilar Incarción, Paula Sanchez, Don Filogonio Perez, Antonio Bustillo, and Agnacio Acosta.

My greatest debt of gratitude is offered to Dawn Southworth, my working partner, who has been indispensable in the preparation of this work in its entirety. The consummate on-location studio manager, she scouted and arranged the details of photographing these interiors, oftentimes letting me know where to place the tripod, and she often provided a final approval on each Polaroid. She has spent months schlepping hundreds of pounds of equipment over thousands of miles over Mexico's rugged terrain, all with two children in tow. She would create an oasis out of our most meager accommodations. From her endless support, our countless conversations, many months on the road together, and her dedication to every aspect of this project, Dawn's presence inhabits these pages in many forms.

To our daughters, Jahna and Simone, thank you for endearing our family unit to new friends south of the border. And thank you for your cheerful dispositions and patient understanding on even those long, hot, and dusty days. I will always treasure the time this project allowed for us to be together.

I am particularly grateful to Barbara Hitchcock at Polaroid for her generous commitment of Polaroid materials at a time when this project was little more than an idea. Her generosity extended throughout the life of this work. I also wish to thank Linda Benedict Jones and Micheala Garzoni at Polaroid. They provided the hundreds of large-format Polaroid images I produced on location, which dramatically enlivened the working process and helped create lasting bonds of friendship.

Three early grants in 1987 funded my initial fieldwork: For a Ruttenberg Fellowship from the Friends of Photography, my thanks to Bill Jay who wrote so insightfully about the work, and to David Ruttenberg; for a Maine Photographic Workshops Photographers' Work Grant, my sincere thanks to Jane Tuckerman, Christopher James, Monica Cipnic, Neil Selkirk, and David Lyman; and for a grant from the Blanche E. Colman Trust, Boston Safe Deposit and Trust Company, Trustee, my thanks to Nicholas Edmonds, Lois Tarlow, Arlette Klaric, Michael Russo, and John Wilson.

I had the honor of working with Peter Timms, director of the Fitchburg Art Museum. We received funding from the Massachusetts Arts and Humanities Contemporary Arts Funding Program, which enabled a meaningful period of fieldwork and research in Mexico, and a subsequent exhibition at the museum of the work-in-progress. My gratitude is extended to Deborah Willis, Dawoud Bey, and John Gossage for their belief in the work.

As the work took on a life of its own, and as the production expenses spiraled upward, I was especially fortunate to receive a John Simon Guggenheim Memorial Fellowship and Subvention. My profound appreciation of this fellowship and its significance at the time cannot be measured. My thanks again to Barbara Hitchcock and Peter Timms, and John Stringer, and Linda Bellon-Fisher for their supportive letters; and to the Committee of Selection for their faith in the project. The principal photography in the states of Chiapas and Michoacán were produced under their auspices. I am also very grateful to Mr. G. Thomas Tanselle, and his assistant Diane Goldberg, at the foundation for facilitating the succeeding Subvention Award, which ensured the publication of this work.

Other significant funding came in the form of a Fulbright Scholar Award, administered through the Council for the International Exchange of Scholars, which enabled my family and me again to spend solid blocks of time focusing upon the spiritual environments created in peoples' homes.

In 1994, additional photography in Chiapas and Guatemala was made possible through support from the Travel Grants Fund for Artists, a joint project of the NEA/Arts International.

Successive annual visits to the island of Janitzio, in Lake Pátzcuaro, Michoacán, for field research, and motion picture and still photography of Mexico's national holiday, El Día de Los Muertos, were funded by the New England Film/Video Fellowship Program of the Boston Film/Video Foundation, through a grant from the National Endowment for the Arts and the Massachusetts Cultural Council; and a New Forms Fellowship from the New England Foundation for the Arts.

For her enthusiasm for this work, and for her encouragement, my heartfelt thanks to Nina Nielsen at the Nielsen Gallery in Boston, who mounted an exhibition of this work-in-progress, introducing this material to a wider audience. A special thanks to Lisa Sette at the Lisa Sette Gallery for her faith in the work and her genuine support, and for bringing the work to the Southwest.

Thanks also to Ivan Karp at the O.K. Harris Gallery; Kathleen Ewing and Charlotte Vazquez at the Kathleen Ewing Gallery; Chris Rauschenberg at Blue Sky; and Gerry McAllister at the University of California San Diego. My appreciation to Meredyth Moses, Terry Etherton, Craig Krull, and Rose Shoshanna for their continued interest. And my gratitude to Howard Yezerski at the Yezerski Gallery in Boston for his thoughtful countenance on many levels.

For their letters in kind support of my work, I wish particularly to thank Jock Reynolds, Susan Stoops, Rod Slemmons, Jeff Rosenheim, Maria Morris Hambourg, Deborah Willis, Arthur Ollman,

Acknowledgments

Alison Devine Nordstrom, Tomas Ybarra Fausto, Trisha Ziff, Robert Seydel, John Jacobs, Alex Harris, David Featherstone, Terrence Pitts, Cliff Ackley, Kenneth Brecher, and Deborah Martin Kao. I am indebted to Jane Livingston for finding a place for me in her unforgiving schedule to write a penetrating and eloquent essay on this work-in-progress.

My gratitude to Ray Scippa and Nancy Mahoney at Continental Airlines for providing travel certificates for many of my flights to Mexico. My thanks to Urlich Krahenbuhl at Sinar Bron Imaging for providing the view camera I used to make many of these photographs. My appreciation to Stan Trecker and Christopher James at the Art Institute of Boston for granting me access to the school's color facilities where I printed the master set of prints for this book. For technical advice while printing, my thanks to Neil Rennie, Carl Mastandrea, Dario Preger, David Akiba, Joseph Bevillard, Mike Boucher, and Jane Tuckerman.

For their friendly advice and opinions on a variety of issues, thanks to Lise and Bill Breen, Roy Ditosti, Bruce Martin, Karen Lukas, Claudia Keel, Walter Bibikow and Claudia Dhimetri, Max Belcher and Ellie Mandell, Ken Brecher and Rebecca Rickman, Rob Amory, Jack and Ali Clift, Julie Bernson, Charles Guliano, Geoffrey Stein, Charlie Barker, Steve Mykolyn, Russell Kaplan and Carolyn Austin, Russell Monk, and Christine Szuter. For joining us in Mexico, thanks to June Southworth, who fostered the family spirit; and to Nancy Wagner and David, Mia, and Chloe Caras; Mary, Tom, Gus, and Timon Cooney; and David Jackson, for their friendship away from home.

Thanks to my parents, Pat and Steve Salvo, for all the extra help and support they have provided. And when Dawn and I traveled alone, special words of thanks to my sister Joyce for being the best aunt on the planet in caring for our children; and to Dawn's mother, June, for being a tireless whirlwind of activity for Jahna and Simone.

My gratitude to Katie Homans for an early book dummy that gave this work promise, and to Sam Antupit, whose dummy provided the spark for Mr. Neurath. At Thames and Hudson my appreciation to Thomas Neurath, whose participation made this publication a reality.

At the University of New Mexico Press, I am particularly grateful to Dana Asbury for her continued interest in this project over many years, and for her sensitive editing and conceptual layout, in which the words and the photographs are true partners in illuminating the history and vitality of Mexico's home altar tradition. Thanks also to Tina Kachele for her thoughtful and elegant design in the creation of this book.

I am greatly indebted to Amalia Mesa-Bains, Salvatore Scalora, William Beezley, and Ramón Gutiérrez for making the cultural and historic context palpable, evoking the climate and spirit in which these photographs were made.

Dana Salvo
January 1997